LUCAS HNATH's plays include *The Christians, Red Speedo, A Public Reading of an Unproduced Screenplay About the Death of Walt Disney, nightnight, Isaac's Eye, Death Tax,* and *The Courtship of Anna Nicole Smith.* He has been a resident playwright at New Dramatists since 2011 and is a proud member of Ensemble Studio Theatre. Awards include the 2012 Whitfield Cook Award for *Isaac's Eye* and a 2013 Steinberg/ATCA New Play Award Citation for *Death Tax.* He is also a recipient of commissions from the EST/Sloan Project, Actors Theatre of Louisville, South Coast Repertory, Playwrights Horizons, New York University's Graduate Acting Program, and the Royal Court Theatre.

A PUBLIC READING OF AN UNPRODUCED SCREENPLAY ABOUT THE DEATH OF WALT DISNEY

"A blackly comic inversion of the public Disney persona, in the form of a stylized screenplay being read in an anonymous-looking corporate conference room . . . Walt would be doing cartoonish gyrations in his grave if he were to see how thoroughly Mr. Hnath (pronounced nayth) has subverted the popular image of Disney."

—Charles Isherwood, *The New York Times*

"Minutes into the darkly humorous play it's clear that for the famous man who made Mickey Mouse, movies and the Magic Kingdom, everything was about him. Always. Especially during his last days on earth."

—Joe Dziemianowicz, *New York Daily News*

"A devastating portrait of a man for whom make-believe was more real than reality itself."   **—Elisabeth Vincentelli, *The New York Post***

"A blood-pumping and often hilarious evening of theater."

—Zachary Stewart, TheaterMania.com

"Enjoyably weird and hermetic . . . Nothing that ever came out of the Magic Kingdom was ever this animated."

—David Cote, *Time Out New York*

THE CHRISTIANS

"Mr. Hnath is quickly emerging as one of the brightest new voices of his generation. What's fresh about his work is how it consistently combines formal invention with intellectual inquiry—both of which are often in short supply in contemporary American theatre."

—Charles Isherwood, *The New York Times*

"*The Christians* is a white-knuckled drama about . . . a theological battle. But there are no clear winners or losers in Lucas Hnath's deeply affecting new play."   **—Elisabeth Vincentelli, *The New York Post***

"For all its control on the page, *The Christians* is about the uncontrollable, which is to say, how we imagine what life will look like once we enter the everlasting." **—Hilton Als, *The New Yorker***

"It's so rare to see religious beliefs depicted onstage without condescension that Lucas Hnath's new play becomes all the more intriguing."
—Frank Scheck, *The Hollywood Reporter*

"Lucas Hnath's soul-searching drama, *The Christians*, grabbed the eyeballs at the 2014 Humana Festival . . . the play's religious dialectic offers enough substance to satisfy true believers."
—Marilyn Stasio, *Variety*

RED SPEEDO

"A bright slip of a swimsuit seems a small garment on which to hang a knotty morality play, but the ingenious Lucas Hnath engineers this remarkable feat with *Red Speedo*, a taut, incisive drama."
—Charles Isherwood, *The New York Times*

"Hnath's swift, slippery play moves in Mametian lunges of rapid dialogue and desperate gambits." **—Adam Feldman, *Time Out New York***

"*Red Speedo* is the latest addition to the increasingly substantial body of work by playwright Lucas Hnath. If you're serious about the theater, you have to see his shows and read his plays and look forward to whatever is next with anticipation. **—Michael Giltz, *The Huffington Post***

"This latest effort similarly reflects the playwright's keen aptitude for exploring hot-button themes."
—Frank Scheck, *The Hollywood Reporter*

"As he did with *The Christians*, Hnath raises hugely important questions about our society and the occasionally perverse behavior it encourages."
—Zachary Stewart, TheatreMania.com

"Hnath lightly suggests—he's too subtle to use the big hammer—that the immoral imbalance of our current economy is stripping us down to our animal skins." **—Jesse Green, *Variety***

THE CHRISTIANS

A PLAY BY
LUCAS HNATH

THE OVERLOOK PRESS
NEW YORK, N.Y.

This edition first published in the United States in 2016 by
The Overlook Press, an imprint of ABRAMS
195 Broadway, 9th floor
New York, NY 10007
www.overlookpress.com

Abrams books are available at special discounts when purchased in quantity
for premiums and promotions as well as fundraising or educational use.
Special editions can also be created to specification. For details,
contact specialsales@abramsbooks.com or the address above.

Cataloging-in-Publication Data is available from the Library of Congress

ISBN: 978-1-4683-1083-2
eISBN: 978-1-4683-1542-4

Book design and type formatting by Bernard Schleifer
Printed and bound in the United States
3 5 7 9 10 8 6 4

This play is dedicated to
Pat C. Hoy, II,
Sarah Lunnie,
and Les Waters

PREFACE

When I was younger, I was supposed to be a preacher, but I decided it would be too much responsibility. I didn't want to worry about other peoples' souls. I switched to pre-med, but I didn't want to worry about other peoples' bodies. And so, I switched to playwriting.

The expectation that I become a preacher did not come out of nowhere. I grew up in churches. My mother went to seminary when I was in middle school. During the summer months I'd sit next to her during her classes. I learned some Greek, some Hebrew. I read books on hermeneutics and epistemology. Some of it I understood. Some of it I pretended to understand.

In seminary you learn a lot about translation. You learn about how there can be more than one way to translate a word. You come to realize just how many words the Bible has that could be translated this way or that way. The act of interpreting the Bible carries with it a lot of responsibility. A friend from high school who ended up becoming a pastor recently said to me that pastors have to be very careful not to remake the gospel into their own image.

But my question was, "Isn't that unavoidable?"

For a few years, I taught expository writing at NYU. I'd have students read challenging texts by folks like Barthes, Berger, or Sontag. I'd ask them simply to read and understand what these writers are saying.

Often the students would project themselves into the meaning of the essays we were studying. The students were eager to find ways to make the texts "relatable," and in doing so, they would bend the words of the author to say something the author isn't actually saying.

That word "relatable" troubles me. It implies that because I think something is like "me" it is therefore generally understandable and also especially good. But what about the things that are nothing like "me"? Our imaginations seem to be so limited by our personal experiences, you have to wonder if it's even possible to understand something that sits outside of those experiences.

That expository writing class became, in large part, about the task of encouraging students to be okay with not immediately understanding the texts. In the rush to understand, we get in the way of our ability to see something as it is.

I can feel that rush to understand when people ask me, with respect to *The Christians*, what I personally believe. I refuse to answer the question. I'm not necessarily cagey about my beliefs (although I do tend to think that the attempt to put those beliefs into words will always result in a misrepresentation of said beliefs; I am very mistrustful of words), but I suspect that answering the question will somehow diminish the effect of the play.

I can also feel it when I'm asked if the play is based on this preacher or that preacher. (Invariably, the answer is no. It's inspired by many different preachers and many people who are not preachers, all thrown into a blender.)

In these kinds of questions, I detect the desire to explain away something. I detect the desire to locate a single, visible "point." And while the plot of *The Christians* is far from ambiguous, the play is a series of contradictory arguments. No single argument "wins." There's no resolution.

That lack of obvious resolution can be uncomfortable, agitating. But we can also take pleasure in the agitation.

And maybe something more complex and true becomes visible within the agitation, amidst the collision of disparate perspectives.

I think back to my very brief pre-med days. I think back to a physics class I took and to a diagram from the course textbook. I think of this diagram often: it depicted a method of seeing a very tiny particle. The particle is too tiny to see with a microscope, but a scientist could detect its presence by colliding it with lots of other particles and studying how those how particles scatter.

Here's what I'm getting at—something I believe very much:

A church is a place where people go to see something that is very difficult to see. A place where the invisible is—at least for a moment—made visible.

The theatre can be that too.

THE CHRISTIANS

PRODUCTION HISTORY

The Christians was commissioned by and premiered in the 2014 Humana Festival of New American Plays at Actors Theatre of Louisville.

The Christians had its Off-Broadway premiere in 2015 at Playwrights Horizons, Tim Sanford, Artistic Director.

WHO
Paul, a PASTOR,
and his WIFE, Elizabeth,
the ASSOCIATE Pastor Joshua,
a church ELDER named Jay,
and a CONGREGANT named Jenny.

WHEN
The 21st century.

WHERE
America.

HOW
In church, a really big church.
And what we see is the stage, raised and carpeted;
in the center, a podium;
and further upstage, hanging, a cross;
surrounding, potted plants;
above, a screen for projections;
off to the side, two or three chairs in a row, chairs for the associate pastors;
and off to the other side, an electric church organ and organist.
Also, a full choir—the bigger the better.
And there are microphones and stands, enough for everyone in the play,
because everyone will always speak on mics, just the way pastors do,
or just the way congregants do when they testify.
The whole play is a kind of sermon.
Sometimes it's a literal sermon.
Sometimes it's made up of scenes that use the formal elements of a sermon.
Occasionally the Pastor narrates to the audience,
which is slightly different from addressing his congregation.

A NOTE ON SONGS

During the play, the Choir will sing four songs. Below are suggestions for what those songs could be. Even if you do not use the suggested song, the song you use should have that general tone. Additionally, the songs you use should not in any way conflict with Pastor Paul's theological stance. It is the responsibility of the producing theatre to obtain the rights to any songs that are not in the public domain.

Song #1—Gospel, steady, comforting, e.g., "God's Unchanging Hand."

Song #2—Faster, rousing, revival music, e.g., "Catch on Fire."

Song #3—A bit anthemic, deliberate, e.g., "I Feel Like Going On."

Song #4—Bright, not-too-fast-and-not-too-slow, e.g. "Farther Along."

ACKNOWLEDGMENTS

Thank you to Sarah Lunnie, Les Waters and Amy Wegener for guiding the play; to Marc Bovino, Phillip James Brannon, Katya Campbell, Rick Foucheux, Marianna McClellan, Dominique Morisseau, Gordon O'Connell, Randy Rand, Thomas Jay Ryan, Kim Schraf, P.J. Sosko for performing in various incarnations of this play; to Emily Donahoe, Andrew Garman, Linda Powell, Larry Powell, Richard Henzel for premiering the play; to Darius Smith and Scott Anthony for musical guidance; to New Dramatists and the Kennedy Center for helping develop the play; to David Collins, Dana Higginbotham, and Mark Schultz for being my theological advisors; to Darlene Forrest and Denice Martone for their support and encouragement; and a very special thank you to Pat C. Hoy, II for the stories.

PRODUCTION NOTES

The Christians was commissioned by and premiered in the 2014 Humana Festival of New American Plays at Actors Theatre of Louisville.

The Christians had its off-Broadway premiere in 2015 at Playwrights Horizons. Artistic Director, Tim Sanford. Directed by Les Waters.

Billing: I am a pagan and proud of it. Believe me,
          before long, we will all be pagans.
Morten: And then will we be allowed to do anything we like?
Billing: Well, you'll see.
                              —Henrik Ibsen, *An Enemy of the People*

I feel an uncontrollable urge to communicate with you,
but I find the distance barrier
                              insurmountable.
                              —Pat C. Hoy, II

(The music plays.)

(The Choir sings Song #1.)

(As this song goes on, enter PASTOR *and* WIFE.*)*

(They join ASSOCIATE *and* ELDER, *already on stage.)*

(The Choir sings Song #2.)

(Singing ends.)

*(*PASTOR *approaches the pulpit.)*

(Takes a microphone in hand.)

PASTOR

Brothers and sisters . . .

Let's pray.

Dear Lord,
bring us together today,
    bring us together
        in our hearts
            and souls
                and minds,

                make us one,
                makes us a body,
                    because when we are one body,
                    we see something
                    we cannot see
                    by ourselves.

Make us whole.
Take away our fear.
Give us strength,
            and give us courage.

Give us the kind of courage that helps us press on
even though we know death is standing there,

watching,

waiting,

give us the courage to know,
to feel,
to understand,
that if we pass through that death, we will find

life

ever
lasting.

In the name
and in the blood
of Jesus.

Amen.

(Pause.)

Today's sermon
has four titles.
If you're taking notes, I suggest you write them down.

They are:

(Titles appear on the screen above.)

Where Are We Today?

A Powerful Urge

The Fires of Hell

and

A Radical Change.

Part 1:
Where are we today?

Well

We   are

          here.

Where is here?

        "Here" is this
            church,
            this big,
            enormous
            building.

            1000s of seats, classrooms for Sunday school,
            a baptismal big as a swimming pool. In the lobby
            there's a coffee shop and a bookstore,
            and out back, a parking lot so vast
            you could get yourself lost in it
            if you're not careful.

Where are we?
      We are here, today,
      a day of celebration,
      a day of freedom . . .

. . . because 20 years ago this church was
nothing more than a storefront church,
10, 15 people.

Then for the next year, every Sunday,
20, 30 people

         and then 50,

and then 100, and 100 that seemed big—

then 500.

We had to move ourselves into a bigger
space, a local gymnasium. But when 500
turned to three times that, then we started
holding three services every Sunday: one at
nine, one at ten-thirty, and one at noon,

and then we grew to twice that,

and then we just couldn't fit.

So,

we built this,
this sanctuary,
built it from the ground up.
And however much we thought it was going to cost,
it cost that and many times over.

And we were in
way over our heads.

That
was ten years ago,
ten years from today.
And you stayed,
and you paid,
and together we prayed
that someday we would finally free ourselves of debt.

And that someday
is today.
And today is the day
that debt is paid.

And ya know, today should be a happy day:
We have, it seems, reason to celebrate.

We have, it seems, reason to think that we are
free.

Sorta reminds me of the one about the man who turned 102,
and at his birthday party,
his friend asked him, "Do you think you'll make it to 103?"
and he said, "Of course I will,
because statistically speaking,
there are very few people who die
between 102 and 103."

But we all know, *a lot* of people die before that.

And we all know, a lot of churches die
before they make it to where we are,
but that doesn't mean
we are as free as we think we are.
There is a different kind of debt
that we have not yet paid

There is—there is a crack
in the foundation of this church,
and I'm not talking about the building.

I'm talking about something like Isaiah talks about,
Isaiah 30, verses 12 and 13:

(The verses appear on the screen.)

"Because you have rejected this Word"—
"this Word," that's God's word he's talking about—
"and relied on oppression

and depended on deceit,
this sin will become for you
like a high wall,
cracked
and bulging,
whose collapse comes suddenly
in an instant."

There is a crack,
and if we don't fix that crack,
it doesn't matter how solid this building is,

    we

        will

            crumble,

    and we will
    fall in on ourselves.

So today we're going to talk a little about that crack,
and we're going to talk about what we have to do
to save ourselves from collapse

(Title appears on the screen: "Part 2: A Powerful Urge")

Twenty-two years ago, I was a young man on an airplane flight from
L.A. to Florida. I'm sitting in my seat, and I see a woman pass me by.
I see this woman, and I think to myself: Lord, that is the most beautiful
woman I have ever seen.

And the Lord said: that's right.

And I said to myself:

    Paul,
    that is the most beautiful woman you have
    ever seen. And my self said to its self: well
    you better do something about it.

And I looked back down the length of the plane and I saw her sitting on the
aisle. She was far away, at the other end of the airplane. Had to lean to see
her, could barely catch her eye. I took out a little scrap of paper, and took out
a pen. And I wrote down,

    "I have a powerful urge to communicate with you,
    but I find the distance between us insurmountable."

I folded the paper, gave the note to the stewardess. I said, "You see that
woman in the pink pantsuit. Will you give this to her." And the stewardess

said yes. And I waited. I watched and I waited and I saw,

> I saw her lean,
>> into the aisle.
>
>> And she looked at me,
>> and she said:
>
>>> *(He waves.)*
>
>> and I said:
>
>>> *(He waves.)*
>
>> And that's all we needed to say, that was it, so easy, so
>> easy you might call it
>
>> grace.

"I have a powerful urge to communicate with you, but I find the distance between us insurmountable."

> *(Pause.)*

(Another title appears on the screen: "Part 3: The Fires of Hell")

> so now —
> I was —
> oh about
> two weeks ago, I was
>
> at a conference for pastors of churches like this church,
> it was a uh conference where you go and hear missionaries
>> speak,
> to hear about the "good"
> work our church is doing in other places.
>
> Now I go to these conferences because
>> I am told to go to these conferences—
> I get a little letter in the mail from the powers that be saying
> you should go to this, and I go, I don't

think about it much—I just go.

And here I am at this conference at the Orlando Marriott,
and I'm eating my free continental breakfast,
and I'm listening to a missionary speak.

This missionary that's talking,
he works overseas in one of those countries
that we hear about on the news,
but if you were asked where it was
or what that country was all about, you probably
wouldn't be able to point to it on a map.

And this missionary, he's trying to start a church there
like the church we have here
in a place—a country—where there's
a lot of fighting, a lot of violence, a lot of chaos,
gun fights and bombs and
and
and
he talks
about one day,
he's in a market,
people going about their business,
shopping, buying food,
and a bomb goes off—I think it was a car bomb.
A grocery store lights on fire.
And people run, they scatter off into—

there's a boy, sixteen, seventeen years old, a young man,
and instead of running away from the burning grocery store,
he runs into it.
He runs into the fire.
And some time passes,
the store is still on fire,
and eventually the boy comes out of the store,
and his whole body is shielding a girl,
        maybe seven years old, this girl—
he's helped her to safety, saved her from the burning building,
but
his own body, is on fire. His clothes are burning,

his arms are burning, his face is
burning, his skin is melting.
He helps the girl to safety,
and she's okay. But
he,
the boy,
is dying.
And there's no one to put out his fire.
And he lies down on the street,
body gone into shock,
and he burns until he's dead.

The missionary tells us that the boy—
that that was his sister that he ran into the store to save.
And the missionary tells us that this boy—he
    didn't know him personally,
but talked to the boy's family enough to know
that the boy was not a Christian.
He did not believe in the God we believe in.
He did not believe in Jesus,
or the Holy Spirit.
He believed in a different set of beliefs,
and attended a church that did not talk about the cross,
and prayed a different set of prayers than the prayers we pray.

And the missionary said, "Isn't it a shame
that we lost that boy, what a man of Christ he might have been."
And and and I thought—
I thought that he meant
"What a shame the boy died," and I thought,
"Yes, what a shame that boy died,"
but the missionary, he meant,
"What a shame, I didn't save this boy for Christ,
what a shame I didn't convert him into a Christian,
what a shame he went to Hell."

The missionary said, "We need help."
He said, "We need money
to save these souls,
we need people,
an' we need your prayers

to save these souls,
because without that,
they all go to Hell."

This boy, by all accounts,
was a good boy.
And yet, he went to Hell.
And what do we say, we say,
"Amen."
And all the pastors at the conference say—they said,
"Amen."

And here I am, thinking about this image,

that boy,
       the body on fire,

and the thought of him
going from one fire
                into another.

I went back to my hotel room that night.
I sat on the toilet, and I cried.

           Convulsively.

              I cried.

I said,
"God, I don't understand."
And he said, "That's not your problem."
And I said,

        "Well it kinda is."
And he said, "Why?"
And I said, "Because I'm a pastor."
And he said, "Oh you're a pastor, what does that mean?"
And he said,

        "No,

no, it's not your problem because
    you haven't made it your problem,
you haven't gone over there and done anything,
you're just sittin' on the toilet."
And I said, "You're right. I am. Just sittin' on the toilet."
And he said, "What are you gonna do?"
And I said, "Well after I'm done here on the toilet,
I'm gonna brush my teeth,
and then I'll go to bed."
And he said, "Why."
And I said—I said . . .
And he said,

"Why."

And I said, "Because you have already done so much."
And he said,

"Exactly."

And he said that he's saved us, he's taken care of us,
    he said, "Why don't you listen when I tell you that?"

And he said, "You think the Devil is a little man with horns."
He said, "You think that?"
An' I said, "I don't know."
An' he said, "You really think that?
        Do you really really really think that?"

And I said, "No,
    not really."
And he said,
"There is no little man.
There is only you
and your fellow man.
You wanna see Satan—?
    there's your Satan.
You wanna see Hell,
    you look around."

And he said, "There is no Hell.
And there is no reason to tell people
that they're going to Hell.

Because they are in Hell.
They are already there.
You gotta take them out of the Hell they're already in.
That boy," the Lord tells me—he says,
"That boy, he is standing next to me right now.
And anyone who tells you otherwise

lies."

      I know
you *all* have a powerful urge to communicate.
I know it. I see it. Your urge
to communicate God's love,
to bring people into this church,
to help them,
to save them
to make their lives better,
and their afterlives

          everlasting.
          You have that powerful urge to communicate.
          But you are failing
          because the distance between
          you
          and everyone else
          is
          insurmountable.

But I'm here to tell you,

      the distance

        is you.

        It's me.

        It's all of us.

        We put the distance there.
        When we shun our neighbors,
        when we judge our friends,
        when we look down at people
        from other places

and other religions,
we create

an insurmountable distance
where there is no distance at all.

Where are we today?
Where are we
today?
I say

we are no longer a congregation that believes in Hell.
A radical change: we are no longer a congregation that
says, "My way is the only way."

We are no longer

that kind of church.

(End of sermon.)

(PASTOR nods to Music Director . . .)

(Organ plays. If there's a band, then the whole band plays.)

(PASTOR sits down.)

(Music plays in silence.)

(A set of projected images play on the wall behind the pastor . . .)

(A lake)

(Majestic mountains)

(A tree in a field)

(The Grand Canyon)

(A dove)

(The sky)

Associate Pastor Joshua will deliver the prayer for the sick,
for those who can't be here today.

Brother Joshua. . .

(ASSOCIATE PASTOR JOSHUA *stands, takes a microphone.*)

(Pause.)

(Then, reading from a list.)

ASSOCIATE`

Please bow your heads in prayer.

Dear Lord,
We bring to you members of the congregation,
who are ill. Their bodies have failed them,
but even so, we know you will not.

We ask that you watch over,
> Jack Rafferty,
> Helen Mounts,
> Abe Jimenez,
> Maxine Judson,
> Peter Stanford,
> Bethany Tallis,
> Sandra Coleman,
> Agnes Silver,
> Herman Santiago,
> Tiffany Leveroux,
> Rachel Stein,
> and Earl Browne.

An' if there are others in our family, who are sick,
who we did not mention,
please look after them too.

> In the name,
> and the power—the cleansing power—
> of the holy blood of Jesus . . .

Amen.

(Music comes to an end.)

(Pause)

(Goes to return to his seat.)

(But then, stops.)

(PASTOR watches.)

(Then he narrates to the audience.)

PASTOR

And we all look at Associate Pastor Joshua.

He just stands there at the pulpit.
I say to him,
"Brother Joshua?"

ASSOCIATE

(Leans into the microphone.)

. . . I find myself

wrestling with your sermon
I . . .

PASTOR

. . .

ASSOCIATE

. . .

PASTOR

(Still very calmly, to ASSOCIATE.)

Go on . . .?

ASSOCIATE

Because what you said in your sermon
seems to go against everything
our church believes.

PASTOR

What do we believe?

ASSOCIATE

We believe in Satan,
and we believe in Satan because the Bible tells us

Satan is

real.

And we believe in Hell,

>because the Bible tells us Hell is there,
>that Hell is the price we pay for sin

PASTOR

>where?

ASSOCIATE

"where" what?

PASTOR

where does the Bible tell us that Hell is waiting for us?

ASSOCIATE

>uhhhhh, seriously?

PASTOR

Yes.

ASSOCIATE

>. . .

PASTOR

>. . .

ASSOCIATE

>in the Bible

PASTOR

yes

ASSOCIATE

>says, "The wages of sin is death."

PASTOR

"Death" is not "Hell"

ASSOCIATE

>means eternal death

PASTOR

says who? says you?

ASSOCIATE

no, the Word of God

PASTOR

show me

ASSOCIATE

when read in context

PASTOR

what context are you referring to?

ASSOCIATE

Luke 16:28

PASTOR

yes—?

ASSOCIATE

(Fumbling with Bible.)

talks about—Jesus he—

let me find it—says . . .

okay

"Let him warn them, so that they
will not also come to this place of torment."

PASTOR

which is

ASSOCIATE

Hell

PASTOR

says "a place of torment"

ASSOCIATE

and that's not Hell?

PASTOR

wouldn't you call guilt, feeling bad about what you've done,
a place of torment?
Isn't that torment enough?

ASSOCIATE

then what about
        Matthew, chapter 10,
                or Luke 12,
                        Matthew 5, verse 22

PASTOR

                                yes— ?

ASSOCIATE

again and again and again, Jesus says, Jesus, He
warns us of Hell, of the danger of Hell, tells us again
and again, about sinners getting thrown into Hell.

Here it's:

PASTOR

                                but it
                                doesn't say "Hell"

ASSOCIATE

are you going to let me read it?

PASTOR

                                sorry
                                go ahead

ASSOCIATE

"Fear God, who has the power to kill you and then throw you into Hell."

PASTOR

It doesn't really say "Hell."

ASSOCIATE
didn't I just say "Hell"?

PASTOR
you said "Hell." But it does not say "Hell."

ASSOCIATE
. . .

PASTOR
In the original language the word "Hell" is not used.
Instead it's "Gehena" and "Gehena" is the name of a
of a garbage dump, a a a place where they burned trash
just outside of Jerusalem.
He was just saying that criminals,
when they die,
often get thrown into that particular trash heap—
which was factually true, so that's
actually what he's talking about.

ASSOCIATE
. . .

PASTOR
. . .

ASSOCIATE
First Corinthians

PASTOR
Congregation, please turn to First Corinthians so you can follow along

ASSOCIATE
15:22

PASTOR
Chapter 15, verse 22,
read along

ASSOCIATE
"For as in Adam all die,"

PASTOR

"For as in Adam *all* die,"

ASSOCIATE

"so also in Christ"

PASTOR

"so also *in* Christ"

ASSOCIATE

"shall all be made alive."

PASTOR

"shall *all* . . . be made alive."

ASSOCIATE

yes

PASTOR

As in Adam we die.

ASSOCIATE

that's what it—yes—it says

PASTOR

but of course we do die, we know that,
we die

ASSOCIATE

but then the "alive" means that it's different

PASTOR

different from whatever it is with Adam

ASSOCIATE

yes

PASTOR

so clearly Christ does something.

ASSOCIATE

It's saying that if you're going to live,
you need Christ

PASTOR

sure

ASSOCIATE

so

PASTOR

so?

ASSOCIATE

And you say, you say this boy,
the boy in the missionary's story,
who uh doesn't believe the Word, doesn't
believe Jesus is the Son of God,
doesn't come from a faith that believes in Christ

PASTOR

that is correct, he did not believe in Christ

ASSOCIATE

so yes, I'm sorry but:
it is certainly,
without a doubt,
a sad and moving story about
what can happen in a fallen world.
But it's just that: a sad and moving story.
It's a message that our work is not done,
and that we need to not be complacent
in these dark end days.

PASTOR

. . .

ASSOCIATE

. . .

PASTOR

So . . .

you're telling me that you would not—if you were—
imagine, you're on the throne, and you have love in your heart—
I know you, I know you have love in your heart—
and this boy comes to you—you will send this boy
to Hell . . .?

ASSOCIATE

I'm not God

PASTOR

no, you're not

ASSOCIATE

blasphemous to even pretend.

PASTOR

I'm asking you
in front of this entire church,
these brothers and sisters,
would you
send that boy to Hell . . . ?

. . . to look that boy in the eyes,
knowing what he has done,
knowing what he has given of himself

ASSOCIATE

. . .

PASTOR

would you

ASSOCIATE

. . . yes

PASTOR

you would

ASSOCIATE

I'd have no choice but to

PASTOR

because—?

ASSOCIATE

it's

PASTOR

what

ASSOCIATE

the law.

PASTOR

Whose law—?

ASSOCIATE

God's.
And God's law is just,
because we are fallen,
an' we are sinful, and we *do*
we *do* go into markets,
and we *do* set off bombs,
and we *do* kill one another.

And in turn, what God asks of us—
all He asks of us—
is to just believe that He is there,
and repent,
and that is so little to ask
to become cleansed—

to say yes, I accept that you sacrificed your Son on the cross,
and we are saved

from Hell.

PASTOR

But

that's not what the Bible actually says,
because according to the verse you just read,
First Corinthians

ASSOCIATE

it says

PASTOR

it says "all," not "some,"

all

ASSOCIATE

who are in Christ

PASTOR

in Christ

ASSOCIATE

with the help of Christ

PASTOR

that he gives

freely.

ASSOCIATE

it says

PASTOR

"*in* Christ,"
interchangeable with "through Christ"
all
through
Christ.

The sentence means:

because of Christ

all are made alive.

First Timothy 4:10:

"we trust in the living God,
who is the Savior of all men,
especially believers."

ASSOCIATE

. . .

PASTOR

"especially believers." Which is to say,
you don't
have to
believe.
It says that—that's
      what
            it
                  actually
         says.

(A beat, a meaningful pause, almost as though ASSOCIATE *really
is checking inside to see what God wants him to do.)*

ASSOCIATE

. . .

PASTOR

. . .

(And then.)

ASSOCIATE

The Lord is tellin me to—in my heart deep down I feel the Lord right now
feel the Lord telling me to—

        reject what you're saying—I feel

PASTOR

yes—?

ASSOCIATE

the Lord is telling me that you are going against His Word

PASTOR

Yes, I got that, Brother Joshua

ASSOCIATE

if you really believe what you say you believe, you are not my brother.

PASTOR

Then

you're free
to leave this church.

I release you.

ASSOCIATE

. . . I don't think I'd be alone

I think there are many who would question your teaching this morning,
who do question—who believe that it is fundamentally against what we
believe.

PASTOR

. . . If that is so, then they can leave
with you.

ASSOCIATE

. . .

PASTOR

(To the audience.)

And Brother Joshua
says:

ASSOCIATE

(Never breaking eye-contact with PASTOR.*)*

Pass around the offering plates.
And have each member of the congregation write down
on a little scrap of paper:
Pastor Paul

or

Associate Pastor Joshua.

Okay?

PASTOR
(To ASSOCIATE.*)*

Okay.

(To the audience.)

And with that,
the ushers pass around the offering plates
to the members of the congregation.

Everyone is taking out pens and little scraps of paper,
and each one writes something down.

And I wait.

(Pause.)

And I think.

(Pause.)

And it takes a long time for this whole process to take place.
And I pray.

(Pause.)

And the offering plates come back,
and Associate Pastor Joshua
and Associate Pastor Ken
and Associate Pastor Will,
my associate pastors count the little bits of paper.

And we wait.

(Pause.)

An' Brother Joshua comes back,
and he is flanked by the two other
associate pastors.

Brother Joshua says,

ASSOCIATE
we have counted the little pieces of paper

PASTOR
(To ASSOCIATE.)
yes. And?

ASSOCIATE
. . . 50

PASTOR
50?

ASSOCIATE
there were 50 people

PASTOR
who said

ASSOCIATE
who sided with me.

PASTOR
okay.

ASSOCIATE
. . . out of the 100s

PASTOR
okay

ASSOCIATE
1000s

PASTOR

I see

ASSOCIATE

who have said
they want
to stay with you.

> *(Pause.)*

> *(Music begins to play. The Choir sings the opening verses of Song #3, then switches into a soft vocalization as* ASSOCIATE *speaks.)*

ASSOCIATE

ya' know, Pastor Paul: many may have sided with you today, but I think there are many more who did not speak up,

many who did not cast their vote, who stayed silent and who do not see things like you see them,

and I imagine there are even people who said they side with you but maybe deep down, they don't.

They just don't want to see you topple when they think you're the one holding up the roof over their heads.

They don't want to see you fall, when they've given so much to you,

given their time, their faith, their money, their trust.

PASTOR

Alright then.

> You've said what you wanted to say.

> Now it's time to go.

> *(The music swells and the Choir sings the closing verses of the song.)*

> *(Silence.)*

(ASSOCIATE *exits.*)

(*All watch as he walks off.*)

(*He's gone.*)

(*Pause.*)

(ELDER JAY *steps forward, takes a mic.*)

(PASTOR *pours himself a glass of water, drinks, and dabs his sweaty brow.*)

(*Silence.*)

(PAUL *finishes his 'rest-and-reset moment'.*)

(*To the audience.*)

PASTOR
And Elder Jay walks into my office and he says,

ELDER
Pastor Paul.

PASTOR
(*To* ELDER.)
Yes, Elder Jay

ELDER
On behalf of myself and on behalf of the church's board of elders . . .

I'd like to take a moment
            and reflect
on your sermon.

PASTOR
go ahead, Brother Jay.

ELDER
You've been a long-time family friend,
            trusted confidante,
                        and spiritual mentor.

An' I just want you to know that

I think this new direction you're taking us is
exciting, it's a—you called it—a radical change and
it's an important change I think for the longer life of our church
and for the life of our faith.

The church board and I, we discussed the sermon, your message, and they
also find it very interesting uh very progressive
what you're doing here.

PASTOR

So you're saying you're behind me

ELDER

yes

PASTOR

you support me

ELDER

yes absolutely

PASTOR

along with the board of this church

ELDER

. . . yes.

PASTOR

well thank you

ELDER

but

PASTOR

oh there's a "but"

ELDER

It's just that as we're celebrating this
new exciting direction for our church community,
I'll be honest: we're really broken up about Joshua leaving this church.

PASTOR

Yes, I know.

ELDER

For the past 5 years he's been a blessing to our family—you do agree that he's been a blessing?

PASTOR

in many ways, yes

ELDER

You've even said yourself that
Joshua is your spiritual son,
that you saved him,
that he walked into this church,
lonely and just looking for some friends.
I seem to remember he was thrown out of his home,
I forget what—some sort of family problems.

And I remember this boy came down to the altar,
saying "I need something
                I don't know what but I need something
                to help me
                        to keep on
                                goin' on."

        And bit by bit,

you gave him more responsibility here at the church:
                a Sunday school class,
                        then counseling responsibilities,
                            the prayer line,
                                then here and there,
                                    Bible reading,
                                        a testimonial in the Sunday
                                            service,
                                        and then you hired him on as
                                            an associate pastor.

        And you'll agree,
        he worked hard

PASTOR

                                        he did

ELDER

he was honest and good and

PASTOR

                        no yes all of that is true Brother Jay

ELDER

he galvanized and organized and revitalized our youth ministries.
You cannot deny he is very charismatic, and gets folks excited
about our church and the work it does.
He became an outspoken member of the community,
going and reaching out
to the poor
and to the sick,
the disenfranchised
and the lost.

PASTOR

. . .

ELDER

So.

What I'm getting at is:
did you have to be so quick to let him go?
Did you have to, need to—was it absolutely necessary to
        cut him off?

While he may have failed to follow you, this time, yes he failed —
he's young, sure, he's got a little chip on his shoulder,

still isn't there room for a second chance
and a third and a fourth and a fifth—?

Your sermon talked about being more accepting,
and so shouldn't that same acceptance be extended to Joshua?

. . . no, I'm going to stop talking and let you speak.

(ELDER does so.)

PASTOR

Thank you for that,
Elder Jay.

I hear you.

Ya' know, it's kinda like a marriage,
how in the Bible it says
that in a marriage
you cannot be unequally yoked.
A divided head cannot lead.
I welcome Joshua into this church.
But if he is going to lead it with me, under me, in any way,
then we need to be
of one mind.
You talk about Joshua
reaching out
being the face of this church
out there in the world.
True: he does reach out.
But what does he show the rest of the world about this church.
How does he represent us.
Do you know how he represents us?

ELDER

I know he can be very uh passionate, sometimes a bit

PASTOR

last November

ELDER

right

PASTOR

you know about this

ELDER

I think I do

PASTOR

Associate Pastor Ken came to me, told me
about how Joshua had gotten together
some of the college kids

ELDER

yes I know this

PASTOR

Saturday nights they'd go downtown,
a group of five or six, they'd
go up to people on the street,
call them out as sinners,
down where the bars are, the clubs,
they'd go up to people and tell them
they were going to Hell, tell them

ELDER

it was inappropriate

PASTOR

How do you think
it makes people feel
to be pulled aside
and told that they're sinners?

ELDER

We're all sinners, aren't we—?

PASTOR

To be told, "Hey—you're bad,
you're a bad person and you should feel bad about yourself."
Why do thieves hang out with thieves?

So they don't feel so guilty.

But shouldn't it be the church that makes a
thief feel welcome.

ELDER
I don't disagree.

PASTOR

But then here we have Joshua and a bunch of college kids calling people sinners, the world looks at us and says, "Who is responsible
    for spreading around all that
                contempt," that's what it is really—
and the world looks back at our church,
and the world looks back at me, me,
and they say, "*He* is responsible for that,"
        and I don't want to be responsible for that,
        that suffering.

            What good is a good church
            if all it does
            is make everyone feel so bad?

ELDER

yes—but what good is a church that no one goes to?

PASTOR

only 50 people left

ELDER

Joshua was very popular, he had a different kind of relationship with the congregation than you, not better, just different, you're so busy running the church, writing your sermons, overseeing all sorts of—I understand that's hard, but that meant Joshua was the one who people came to, who listened, on a daily basis, to their problems. He was the one that people had a uh uh more personal relationship with—again, you're busy, you can't be blamed, but I have to think that carries a certain weight. I just think that Joshua served a very important function and without him

PASTOR

you think

ELDER

yes

PASTOR

or the board thinks—?

ELDER

I'm just here to let you know their concerns

PASTOR

and I need you to tell the board that there's nothing to be concerned about.

ELDER

We can't afford a schism

PASTOR

afford

ELDER

yes

PASTOR

now you're talking about money

ELDER

among other things

PASTOR

the church has paid its debt

ELDER

only to incur another?

PASTOR

You and the board worry about the business of the church so that I don't have to.

ELDER

. . . well, you say that, Paul, but you have a board, a group of
ten or so people who really like you a lot,
and care about you and your ministry,
and your family, and they wouldn't be serving on the board
unless they cared about you.
And keep in mind, we're—we're not business-minded,
I mean I'm a doctor, I give out flu shots; Jerry, our treasurer, runs a
local telemarketing firm, and
we have
no prior experience running something on this scale,
this church, you understand, it's a massive corporation, and
for the past several years while the church was in debt, that was scary,

for sure, and in the middle of it all, when Agnes got caught on
the church escalator, got her leg all cut up, turns out the board of
directors was personally liable, and we had to get lawyers—we're
in the position where we do have our necks on the line in a way
that you don't. You understand.

PASTOR

I do.

ELDER

But at same time, we had a congregation that was here every Sunday
and was growing, exponentially and so
slowly but surely, the place got paid off.

I worry, yes, I do worry, a little, about what happens when you tell a congregation that they don't need to believe— then I have to wonder if that
makes them feel like going to church isn't so important.

PASTOR

So would you have me threaten them—?

ELDER

no

PASTOR

would you have me tell them that if they don't come to church,
they're going to Hell—?

ELDER

no

PASTOR

would you have me tell them that if they don't tithe every week,
they'll burn—?

ELDER

oh no of course not

PASTOR

then what would you have me say
that I'm not already saying?

(The Choir sings Song #4, abruptly ending the scene.)

(At the end of the song . . .)

(JENNY, a Congregant and a member of the Choir, steps forward and takes a mic.)

(She looks to PASTOR and says . . .)

CONGREGANT

Pastor Paul, I'd like to give a testimonial

PASTOR

(To CONGREGANT.)
thank you sister Jenny

CONGREGANT

I'm gonna read if that's okay

PASTOR

that's fine.

CONGREGANT

(Reads from a piece of paper.)
Pastor Paul.
Sister Elizabeth.
I really wanna just thank both of you.
You two have been such a blessing to me and my family,
which right now,
consists really of just me and my son, Donny.

Over the past seven or so years you and this church family
has been there with me through some pretty tough times.
When I got divorced, you and your associate pastors
counseled with me.
And when my husband refused to pay alimony,
you helped us get food stamps.
You let us use the church clothing bin,
so that my son would have new clothes to wear
when school starts in the fall.

And when I feel sad and like I'm gonna collapse,
it does something for me to walk into this building.

There's a spirit in the building that is really something special,
like the spirit of God is in this place,
and it makes me feel like I can go on one more day.

It's been really great to sit here and listen to the testimonials that church
members have delivered in response to your sermon.
They said some really beautiful things.

       and you know . . .

I've been thinking a lot about the sermon you preached,
and I think what you said about this church,
and the walls of this church, how we've built up walls,
how we have cut ourselves off from the world.

And what you said about distance and communication,
and what you said about Hell,
how the Bible says, in a lot of ways, that there is no Hell,
and that through Christ all are saved,
and yes,
       all of that makes sense.

It makes me really sad that people left the church
because of what you preached.
Some of those who left are really close friends of mine.
Those friends—I feel like they look at me
differently than they used to look at me.
I call them up, ask them to get coffee with me, and they don't.
They're too busy.
And before they hang up, they say they're praying for me like there was
    something wrong with me.

PASTOR
. . . sorry to hear that, sister Jenny

CONGREGANT
*(Nods, almost inaudibly says "thank you," maybe off mic. Beat.
Continues reading.)*
an' it makes me feel judged and bad,
and I think this is the thing you were trying to fix with your sermon,
but in some ways it made it worse.

I don't know how to respond to them
when they ask me questions that I don't have answers to.
A lot of us are getting asked a lot of the same questions from the
people who left and went to the new church that Brother Joshua
started.

They point to other Bible verses where it doesn't sound like Hell
is just a trash dump. Like for example, there's one where Jesus
talks about your soul being burned in the thing you're calling a
trash dump and it makes me wonder if it's a real trash dump
then how does it burn a soul. It's as if you have a choice about
how to read it.

And my kid asks me questions, about how what we believe
could just so suddenly change. And when he asks me, then I get
nervous because I see myself as leading him. I pick the church
we go to, and so in a way I'm really responsible for his soul. Our
lives are hard enough already, I don't need to be jeopardizing
the spiritual well-being of my son.

And then this guy I was seeing, a guy I met last November in
singles group, just last week he left and went to Brother Joshua's
new church. He's been asking a lot of questions.

I try to defend you when he asks me about it,
He says things like, "Well if there's no punishment,
why should we be good?"
And I say, "We are good because we know that's right,
because if we're just being good
because we're scared of getting in trouble,
that's not really being good."
And then he says, "But if there's no punishment for being a sinner,
isn't that a slap in the face to those who are good?"
But then I'm like, "That's not our problem—worrying about
     whether or not other people are getting punished."

PASTOR

I think that's a very good answer, Jenny, I—

CONGREGANT

(Takes the mic in her hand.)
And then the guy, he asked me,

> "What about someone like Hitler,
> if there's no hell,
> then what about him.
>
> Where does he go?"

That's a real question—I'm asking for an answer.

PASTOR

. . .

CONGREGANT

. . .

PASTOR

. . .

CONGREGANT

. . .

PASTOR

so

now see

if all are saved through Christ

all

then so is Hitler, so must even he be
Hitler is in Heaven.

The thief on the cross next to Jesus is in Heaven,
     Hitler is in Heaven,
          and everyone in between,
          and everyone who comes after.

CONGREGANT

see now, that's hard to swallow, I think

PASTOR

if there is no Hell

CONGREGANT

can't he just go nowhere?

PASTOR

But then you have to figure out where the line is,
how do you draw that line?

CONGREGANTT

but according to you, it sounds like God doesn't even draw lines

PASTOR

no yeah I don't think he does.

CONGREGANT

What you're basically saying is that if someone were to
murder my son

PASTOR

yes

CONGREGANT

and the murderer dies

PASTOR

yes

CONGREGANT

then both my son and the murderer would be in Heaven together.
And me too, when I die, all three of us
like a like a big happy family

PASTOR

. . . yeah

that's right.

But I mean . . .

think about it

wouldn't that be Heaven—?

CONGREGANT

no

PASTOR

a place where everything that was awful about earth is gone,
where the wrong that one has done is washed away,

isn't that Heaven?
Wouldn't you want that too: no matter what you've done, it can all be
washed away?

CONGREGANT

I can't imagine it, that Heaven,

and if I can't imagine it, I can't believe it,
and if I can't believe in Heaven,
then that makes me feel lonely
and scared.

PASTOR

. . . But

why?

CONGREGANT

Why what?

PASTOR

I just . . . I don't understand
    your need to—
    please don't take this the wrong way but
    I don't understand why Heaven should be imaginable.
    I think I would be disappointed if Heaven
        were something I could imagine,
    because what I can imagine is pretty dull, it's pretty uhhh

imaginable. I want the Heaven
  that my mind cannot fathom,
  that is better than what my human brain can handle.
I want a God who doesn't think like a man,
  who isn't as small-minded as I am,
  who is, in a way, unearthly and inhuman.
Because I'd be pretty scared and feel pretty lonely
if God were so
              imaginable.

            You see?

            So my advice to you
            is to be patient.
            To sit with it.
            To pray.
            To have an open heart.
            And the understanding
                      will come.

            Okay?

CONGREGANT
            Okay

PASTOR
            Thank you, Jenny.

CONGREGANT

just

        one other thing I don't understand

PASTOR
                      mm-hm

CONGREGANT
        (She won't look PASTOR *in the eyes.)*
another thing the guy I was seeing said to me.
And I didn't like that he said it
but it stuck with me

and it left me wondering why
you preached that sermon when you did.
He said he just wondered why,
you did this after,

just after

the church paid off its debt.
It just seems that—he said, he thought—the timing
seemed too convenient.
That if you had done this before the church was paid off
and people had left, then you'd be in a bad spot.

And he said he feels taken advantage of

PASTOR

I never

CONGREGANT

and he—he feels like you took our money.

PASTOR

no

CONGREGANT

he wanted to know—I'm going back to reading here—
      (Reads.)
why you did what you did when you did it,
because he thinks that what you said about Hell
couldn't have been something that just occurred to you,
that you must have known for a long time
that "Hell" is Greek for "trash dump,"
that you didn't just figure that out,
which means you had this thought
but had been preaching something different—
which seems to me kinda like lying sorry to say that—
and then you suddenly decided
that once the church was paid off,
you could risk losing money,
and tell us what you really thought.

Is that it?

PASTOR

. . .

CONGREGANT

. . .

PASTOR

I don't think I ever really talked about Hell in my sermons

CONGREGANT

because you never believed in it to begin with?

PASTOR

. . .

CONGREGANT

. . .

PASTOR

I had questions, I had doubts about it.

CONGREGANT

So why didn't you tell us that earlier

PASTOR

what would I have said?

CONGREGANT

that you're not certain about certain things we believe

PASTOR

would that have made you feel better, to hear me get up here and say that I don't know?

CONGREGANT

I just can't help but feel used, Pastor Paul, I don't have much money, I give twenty percent every week, I live on food stamps and out of clothing bins, and it's a big deal, I don't do the minimum ten percent, I go over that, because this church is really important to me and giving to God is important, and there's so much that me and my son have had to do without because of it.

PASTOR

. . .

CONGREGANT

. . .

PASTOR

I'm sorry

CONGREGANT

for what?

PASTOR

that you feel the way you feel.

I'm sorry.

CONGREGANT

. . .

PASTOR

can we

can the church help you in some way

CONGREGANT

how? I don't—

PASTOR

give you some money, some assistance

CONGREGANT

why?

PASTOR

you seem to be under the impression that I'm preoccupied with money, and I'd like you to understand that I don't care about the money, that I don't—

CONGREGANT

are you trying to pay me off?

PASTOR

No, no, not at all the idea is to

CONGREGANT

why—is it guilt?

PASTOR

to show appreciation for what you've given, the idea is to give back a blessing

CONGREGANT

What I want is for you to tell me the truth

PASTOR

I am.

CONGREGANT

no lying—not in this church, not at this pulpit

PASTOR

I don't.

CONGREGANT

this business about Hell, would you have brought it up, before the church was paid for?

PASTOR

. . .

CONGREGANT

. . .

PASTOR

(*After a moment of really searching for the answer . . .*)
God had not yet told me to deliver that message

CONGREGANT

so you're saying you never thought about how that sermon could maybe make it so the church wasn't paid off, you're telling me that you never worried about it, never crossed your mind.

PASTOR

. . .

CONGREGANT

. . .

PASTOR

no, I'm not saying that.

CONGREGANT

. . .

PASTOR

I do make decisions based on what's best for the church. I try to make decisions based on—I think about what the congregation is ready for, and when they're ready for it

CONGREGANT

how do you know what I'm ready for and what I'm not ready for, what gives you that—

PASTOR

in my heart—I felt that we needed to overcome one hurdle before we took on another—and I do think about—it's not just about me—we have a board of directors—they handle the business of the church—I don't—and it's an enormous burden, right Elder Jay?

ELDER

. . .

CONGREGANT

I just want a good answer is all,
because that guy I was dating,
he made a lot of good points,
and I don't know what to say back to him.

PASTOR

. . .

CONGREGANT

. . .

PASTOR

. . .

CONGREGANT
(Off-mic.)
you gonna say anything?

PASTOR

. . .

CONGREGANT

. . .

PASTOR
(Maybe half off-mic.)
I I I see how you um—

CONGREGANT

. . .

PASTOR

. . .

(And the silence goes on for a bit.)

(PASTOR is awkward.)

(But CONGREGANT waits for an answer.)

(But then she lowers her head, she nods.)

CONGREGANT
okay, I guess I'm gonna go.

PASTOR

. . .

CONGREGANT

. . .

PASTOR

. . .

(And she goes . . .)

(ELDER stands and exits.)

(And then the Music Director goes, too.)

(And then the Choir.)

(PASTOR turns back and looks at WIFE, regards her.)

(Long pause.)

(To the audience.)

and I look at my wife and I say,

hey

(Pause.)

(WIFE takes a mic.)

WIFE

hey

(Pause.)

PASTOR

I say,

how're you holdin up there?

WIFE

I'm not sure

PASTOR

she says,

WIFE

I think more people just left our church

PASTOR

and she says,

WIFE

maybe

PASTOR

she says,

WIFE

maybe it's not such a good idea to talk about Hitler.

PASTOR

And we lie in bed,
and I think, and she asks,

WIFE

what are you thinking

PASTOR

and I say

(To WIFE.*)*

I'm thinking
about that woman

WIFE

what woman

PASTOR

that woman Jenny, the woman who

WIFE

thinking what about her?

PASTOR

. . . Did she go to your Women's Bible Study group?

WIFE

she did

PASTOR

and she had all those questions

WIFE

yes, she did

PASTOR

and it sorta made me wonder if she ever asked you

any of the questions she asked me,
and made me wonder if you ever tried to answer those questions,
and if you did, I found myself wondering what you said
to try to answer those questions.

I'm not suggesting you did anything wrong, or any of what happened was
your fault

WIFE
oh no, I know

PASTOR
I'm just curious.

WIFE
No.
     She never asked me any of those questions.

PASTOR
and have others—?

WIFE
have others what—?

PASTOR
asked those questions or similar questions
to the questions Jenny asked—
have other women in your Women's Bible Study group,
          ya know, since I delivered that sermon,
have others come to you with
similar questions
and concerns?

WIFE
          Yes.

PASTOR
                              And what do you tell them?

WIFE
          I tell them that if they have questions about something you've
said,

then they should ask you,

> not me.

PASTOR

> oh, okay.

WIFE

Because I don't want to put words in your mouth

PASTOR

oh sure,
thank you, I, no, yeah, that's—I appreciate that,

> but I was also thinking,

> > maybe you could—

> I wouldn't mind if you

> fielded some of those questions, I
> > wouldn't take it as you putting words in my
> mouth, I think it helps to hear answers coming from you,
> not just from me, it shows
> that we're in this together.

WIFE

right

PASTOR

and you're such a gifted communicator

WIFE

thank you

PASTOR

And I think
if you were to speak
to the women in your group,
it could do a lot to help,
to help them see the value
in what I'm talking about.
I think it could help keep

more people from leaving the church—
it's startin' to feel sorta like our church has sprung a leak

WIFE

you want me to help plug up the leak

PASTOR

I could help you, prepare a message for you,
show you the verses that will help them understand
what I'm saying.

WIFE

. . . but what if it's better that the people who are leaving just go ahead
and leave if they're not inclined to go along with the change

PASTOR

I think they just don't understand the change

WIFE

what is there to understand?

PASTOR

I don't want people to leave

WIFE

there were some you wanted to see go

PASTOR

of course not

WIFE

you were happy to see Joshua go

PASTOR

okay well

WIFE

you've been wanting him to leave for a long time,
you and Joshua had been preaching different things.

PASTOR

it was a problem that needed fixing

WIFE

and those 50 who sided with him,
those 50 who sided with Joshua,
you were also happy to see them go.

Come on now, admit it.

PASTOR

in order for a tree to grow
some pruning is necessary

WIFE

an amputation so that the rest of the body doesn't get infected.

PASTOR

yeah, it's sorta like that.

WIFE

you're saying that absolute tolerance requires intolerance of the intolerant.

PASTOR

It depends on the circumstances.

WIFE

So—

. . . what if I were to tell you
that when the offering plates went around,
the little piece of paper I put into the plate
said Joshua
and not Paul

PASTOR

. . .

WIFE

. . .

PASTOR

. . .

WIFE

. . .

PASTOR

is this a hypothetical question?

WIFE

no.

PASTOR

oh.

WIFE

. . .

PASTOR

. . .

WIFE

Should I be amputated as well?

PASTOR

uh, no.

WIFE

are you sure about that

PASTOR

yes

WIFE

Because I believe in Hell.
I believe in the Devil.
I believe that believing in Jesus,
believing that He's the Son of God,
and believing that He died for your sins
is the only,
the *only* thing that can secure you a place in Heaven.

PASTOR

Why didn't you tell me earlier that you disagreed with my sermon?

WIFE

Why didn't you tell me earlier that you were going to deliver that sermon?
Why didn't you tell me that you were going to forcibly
      change
           what our church
               believes?

PASTOR

. . .

WIFE

In your sermon you talked like you had been struggling with this message, tormented,
but you never told me any of that.

PASTOR

I don't normally check my sermons with you

WIFE

And I think it's kind of too bad that you don't.

I think what you did
      was actually
           incredibly selfish

PASTOR

selfish?

WIFE

yeah

PASTOR

how???

WIFE

You haven't thought about
how what you're doing affects other people.

PASTOR

Everything I'm doing is about other people.

WIFE

What about me? What about our daughter?

PASTOR

what about her

WIFE

you know that most of her classmates go to our church

PASTOR

okay

WIFE

and some of the parents of some of those classmates
talk about you in front of their kids.
And the kids come to school,
tell her that her daddy is going to Hell.
Did you know that?

PASTOR

no

WIFE

and she doesn't know what to do,
she wants to stand up for you,
but doesn't know how.

PASTOR

How would I have known about that?

WIFE

if you just opened up your eyes and paid attention
    to the people around you

PASTOR

you hide things from me. All the time you—

WIFE

you never consulted with me,
never told me that you were struggling with something.
That tells me, I'm not on the same level as you.

You don't see me as someone you would
  talk to about the things you're thinking,
                that I'm just the preacher's wife,
                that I just sit in the background,
                just nod my head,
                and support you in every decision you make.

                                        I'm not that kind of
                                         preacher's wife

PASTOR

I know you're not.

WIFE

I think you figured that if I experienced your amazing sermon
with the rest of the church, I'd be all swept up with all the rest of them,
and just buy into it on account of your own magnificence.

PASTOR

I don't think I'm magnificent!

WIFE

        But Paul, it didn't work on me,
        and for those for whom it did work,
        your magnificence is starting to wear off.

PASTOR

    (To the audience.)
    and she says,

WIFE

It feels so
strange, that
almost overnight,
you don't have the same beliefs as me.

PASTOR

    (To WIFE.)
Our beliefs are mostly the same

WIFE

no, no they're not

PASTOR

(To the audience.)
and she says,

WIFE

and I wonder what else you believe,
that I don't believe,
that I don't know about yet,
that would scare me to know you believe.

And when will I find out about that.

And then I wonder if someday
you'll convince me of what you believe.
And then I sit here and I think about me,
a version of me, say, two years from now.

And she believes what you believe,
and she believes what I don't believe, not right now.
I think about that future "me,"
and I think about that future "me" thinking about the
"me" I am right now.
That version of me thinks I'm stupid for thinking what
I think now,
but also,
I'm here thinking that she's so wrong,
and I don't want to think something so different from
what I think now . . .

. . . because there's a slipping that happens.

PASTOR

and she says,

WIFE

I feel so alone right now,
because where you are is so different from where I am.

PASTOR

(To WIFE.)
I'm sorry.

I'm sorry.
You're right.
I should have told you—
I think I . . .

WIFE

The way I see it, I have one of two options.
My sister said I could stay with her,
indefinitely. I figured I could go there,
our daughter would come with me, we'll go for a visit,
and then figure out from there where to go,
what to do.

Or,

I stay

PASTOR

well I think that's the option I'd prefer

WIFE

and I continue the Women's Bible Study

and preach what you're not preaching.
Use my ministry as a, I dunno, a platform,
a pulpit, not sure what to call it—
for correcting what you're saying

PASTOR

correcting?

WIFE

balancing things out, I guess.

PASTOR

seems like that would tear apart the church even worse than it already is.

WIFE

. . .

PASTOR

What do I do—? what do you want me to do—?

WIFE

what I want you to do
I don't want you to do because I want you to do it.
I want you to do something
because you want to do it,
because you believe it,
and I think that *is* what you're doing now,
and that's the problem.

PASTOR

I'm doing what I think God has told me to do.

WIFE

Me too.

PASTOR

Do you still like me?

WIFE

. . . I do still like you.

PASTOR

Do you still . . . find me attractive?

WIFE

I do.
. . . Do you still find me—?

PASTOR

Of course

WIFE

you

PASTOR

yes

WIFE

well that's nice

PASTOR

you're very attractive

WIFE

good to know.

But

I wish I didn't.
I wish I didn't like you,
I wish I didn't find you so attractive,
I wish I didn't want you here in bed beside me,
I wish I didn't think that you're so smart
   and kind
     and good,
and I wish I didn't find you so magnificent.
Because if I didn't feel all those ways
it would be so easy to—

I'm worried that we won't be together forever,
and I'm worried that it'll be my fault,
and God will say—when it comes time to say the things he'll say—
"Why did you fail him?"
"Why did you let him fall away?"
"Why did you not do everything you could to keep him from falling away?"

And so this is me, doing everything I can do,
but really, I'm afraid to do everything that I could do,
but I know I have to do everything I can do,
because I want to be with you forever.

   By staying with you, I am making it easier.
    Aren't I?
      It would be harder if I weren't here.

PASTOR

. . .

  *(*WIFE *exits.)*

  (Enter ASSOCIATE.*)*

ASSOCIATE

They say

they say that people don't attend the church anymore

PASTOR

attendance went down.

ASSOCIATE

They say your wife is leaving you.

PASTOR

where did people hear that—?

ASSOCIATE

they say your daughter is having a rough time at school

PASTOR

she's doing better.

ASSOCIATE

They say the church has gone back into debt

PASTOR

we've hit a rough patch

ASSOCIATE

unable to pay for its staff

PASTOR

no, I've been paying folks out of my own savings

ASSOCIATE

unable to pay for the lights

PASTOR

okay well.

ASSOCIATE

They say—

The church's board of elders—they said to me, "Will you come back?"
I said, "I don't want to come back,"
they said, "Please think of coming back,"
I said, "No way,"
they said, "No,

        no, we're not asking you to come back as associate pastor.
        We're asking you to come back
                as head pastor."

PASTOR

. . . When did this happen—?

ASSOCIATE

A couple of days ago.
They said, "Don't tell Paul,"
I said, "So you haven't said to him what you said to me?"
They said, "No."

I said, "That's not right."
I said, "I don't feel comfortable discussing this
if he doesn't know what I know."
I said, "It feels like I'm going behind his back."

I said, "I'm gonna tell him."
They said, "Don't."
I said nothing.

I thought you should know.

(Pause.)

PASTOR

Are you going to accept?

ASSOCIATE

What would I be accepting?

The people who stayed here wouldn't have me.

You have characterized me
as being hateful
as being judgmental
as being

a bad Christian.

PASTOR

No, I don't think I have

ASSOCIATE

many people have told me

PASTOR

I . . . never speak specifically about you

ASSOCIATE

I walk down the aisle here,
and the people who stayed
look at me with a look that says I am not welcome here.

PASTOR

I think that's all in your head.

ASSOCIATE

You've made it out to sound like
what I believe is a cartoon Hell
with cartoon devils,
pitchforks and

well when you make it look like that,
it's hard to take what I say seriously.

You make it sound like what I want is to see people punished

PASTOR

well do you?

ASSOCIATE

You make it sound like I want to believe there is a Hell.

PASTOR

I think you're choosing to believe in it

ASSOCIATE

choosing

PASTOR

yes.

ASSOCIATE

It's not easy for me to believe in Hell.

PASTOR

Are you sure about that?

ASSOCIATE

I think for you, being a Christian is easy

PASTOR

no, it's hard, it's really—

ASSOCIATE

Your parents were Christians,
your parents' parents—
everyone took you to church,

and everyone wanted to see you saved,
and for you, you had nothing to lose
by believing what you believed.

But ya know, I lost everything.
My parents—they didn't believe
in what I believe.

I tried. Again and again, I tried
to bring them to Jesus,
wanted nothing more,
right up until the end,
I tried.
So that my mother, when she died,
I was there in the hospital,
standing by her side,
telling her about Jesus,
telling her what Jesus did for me.
I asked her, "Please please
hear what I have to say,
open your heart, just a little."
And she said, "Baby, I don't like how you sound
when you preach at me,"
she said, "When you talk Jesus talk,
you don't sound like you."
And I said, "That's cuz I'm filled with the spirit."
And she said, "No it's just creepy is all."

I said, "This is your last chance."
I said, "Mama, listen:

any moment now, you're gonna go,
and when you do,
I will never get to see you again."
I said, "In the coming age, after I have also left this earth,
if you die a believer
we will be reunited,
and we will live together in eternity."
I said, "Mama, don't you want to see me again?"
And she said, "Yes, baby, yes, baby,
of course, I want nothing more."
And I said,
"Then just say you believe, say it with me, say
'I believe in Jesus, and I believe
He died for my sins,' say it with me,"
and she said,
"I would like to say I believe,
but if I did it would be a lie"
I said,
"But maybe that's enough—
Say you believe in the hope that
as you say you believe you will believe
and maybe you'll truly believe."
And she said,
"Honey, I am going, I am leaving this earth,
and I will not spend my final breath,
sayin' a damn lie,"
and she said, "When I close my eyes,
my eyes won't open again.
And when I close these eyes,
I'll see black,
and there will never again be
anything but."

And I said, "Please please please."
And she said nothing.
And in a couple of seconds her eyes would
close . . .

But before her eyes closed and closed for good,
there was a moment,
a moment that was terror,

dread,
pain—
our eyes connected, and she saw me seeing her

fall,

and at that moment, her hand reached out
and grabbed my wrist, like she was grabbing for help.

It's not easy for me to believe there is a Hell.
And it doesn't make me feel good.
In fact, it hurts, because I know,
             every day,
that I will never see my mother again,
and if I do, it will be me, high above her,
             looking down,
             seeing her suffer

                              for the rest of eternity.

An' I wonder sometimes—Pastor Paul—if my Heaven
   will be a kind of Hell.

PASTOR

. . .

ASSOCIATE

so just

         show me.

PASTOR

. . .

ASSOCIATE

Show me.

Show me.

Show me that there is no Hell, show me,
   don't play word games with the Bible, show me and
and

and I'll come back to this church, not as a head pastor
   but as your associate, and I'll support

you and your message, just show me that what I saw I didn't see,
because when my mother died, I did—I saw it—

I saw it, I felt it, I saw firsthand
what Hell looks like,
and nothing can take that away from me, so
what business do I have
preaching the possibility that it doesn't exist.
I'd be leading hundreds,
thousands,
into hell
while setting aside for myself something even worse
for bein some kinda
false shepherd.

PASTOR

. . .

ASSOCIATE

. . .

PASTOR

I can't show you the absence of something.

ASSOCIATE

well then,
there we have it

PASTOR

(To the audience.)
he says,

ASSOCIATE

I'm not accepting the offer

PASTOR

he says,

ASSOCIATE

the elders will have to find someone else to take your job

PASTOR

he says,

ASSOCIATE

I've got my own church now

PASTOR

(To ASSOCIATE.*)*
I hear it's doing really well

ASSOCIATE

we hold services in a
YMCA

PASTOR

the one off of

ASSOCIATE

17

PASTOR

not a bad spot.

ASSOCIATE

The bathroom situation could be better,
and the microphones they've got there
tend to give a lot of feedback.
But I make it work

PASTOR

I bet you do

ASSOCIATE

I tend to just use my own voice instead.
It carries.

I'm praying for you, brother.

(Exit ASSOCIATE.*)*

(And then . . .)

PASTOR

fewer people in church this week than the last,
    this year fewer
        and next year even fewer.

I wonder

    I wonder

        might be a time,
            when

        there are no more Christians.

And will people believe what we believe
    100
        1,000
            10,000 years from now?

Many religions have died.

            now—why do I believe what I believe

I believe what I believe because I know it is true—but why do I know it's
true?—it's a feeling. And where did that feeling come from?—God. God
put it there—but how do I know it's God that put it there?—I know it's God
because I believe God is there—but how do I know God is there? because there's a feeling he put inside of me—but
What if I were different?
What if I had a different family
and was raised differently,
not taken to church . . .?
        But I was taken to church, and
I had the family that I had,
and they raised me to believe that the feeling I feel is from God,
        but what if this—?
        and what if that—?
        but no—what didn't happen didn't happen
            because God made it that way.

(WIFE *re-enters.*)

WIFE

. . .

PASTOR

(*To* WIFE.)
I have a powerful urge to communicate

but I find the distance between us

insurmountable.

WIFE

I think back to me
        and my younger self
        on an airplane flight from California to Florida.
I think back to the handwritten note
        handed to me by the stewardess.
I think back to me
        looking out
        and down the aisle,
        and seeing a handsome man waving at me.
And I think back to me
        in that moment
        hearing a voice that sounded like God
        saying that's the man
        you'll spend the rest of your life with.
But sometimes,
        sometimes it's really hard
        to really know
        which voice is God
        and which one is your own wishful self.

PASTOR

Be patient with me,
and stay a little longer.

WIFE

My bags are packed.

PASTOR

They can stay packed.

WIFE

We're losing the church

PASTOR

Which means you're all I have.

WIFE

We might not be together forever.

PASTOR

Then shouldn't we spend together what time we know we have.

WIFE

. . .

PASTOR

Don't worry about trying to figure it out now.
It will make more sense later.

WIFE

. . .

(Lights out.)

(End of play.)

ALSO BY LUCAS HNATH

RED SPEEDO

Ray's swum his way to the eve of the Olympic trials. If he makes the team, he'll get a deal with Speedo. If he gets a deal with Speedo, he'll never need a real job. So when someone's stash of performance-enhancing drugs is found in the locker room fridge, Ray has to crush the rumors or risk losing everything. A sharp and stylish play about swimming, survival of the fittest, and the American dream of a level playing field—or of leveling the field yourself.

A PUBLIC READING OF AN UNPRODUCED SCREENPLAY ABOUT THE DEATH OF WALT DISNEY

It's about Walt's last days on earth. It's about a city he's going to build that's going to change the world. And it's about his brother. It's about everyone who loves him, and how sad they're going to be when he's gone. Can Walt control the future from the grave? Why does his daughter hate him so much? Were thousands of lemmings harmed in the making of a famous Disney nature film? Stay tuned...

THE OVERLOOK PRESS · NEW YORK · WWW.OVERLOOKPRESS.COM